# How to Jump and Spin on In-Line Skates

# How to Jump and Spin on In-Line Skates

By
Jo Ann Schneider Farris

With additional material by Marion Ennis Curtis

Illustrations by Larisa Gendernalik

ISBN # 1-58721-052-5

1$^{st}$ Books rev 9/15/00

This book is dedicated to my parents.

Thank you for giving me skating.

Thank you for encouraging me.

Thank you for loving me.

# Acknowledgements

I would like to thank the following people who helped with this writing: roller skating coaches Larry Bishop and Stacey Lavender, who both encouraged me to try moves I did not think were possible on in-line skates and helped me to understand more about roller skating; Shirley, David, Shane, Sarina, and Melissa Hayden and Frankie Bishop, owners/managers of Bosanova Roller Skating Center in Colorado Springs, who made me feel so welcome at their facility; ice skating coach and colleague Larisa Gendernalik, who encouraged me and illustrated most of this project; (Larisa wants me to mention that at the time she began jumping and spinning on in-lines, she was 44 years old – so remember, you are never too old to jump and spin on in-line skates!); Chelsee and Michelle Foster, who took the time to allow me to take photos of Chelsee; skater Nathalie Biedermann and photographer Eric Maurer of Visiomatics (www.skatetrix.ch) for giving me permission to share their wonderful photos of Nathalie; my editors Bruce Curtis and Susan Grimm for their time and dedication to detail, and my lifelong friend, Marion Ennis Curtis, for her support and encouragement. I'd also like to thank Harmony Sports, John Petell and Nick Perna for inventing the *PIC®* Frame Skate!

# Table of Contents

# Why Jump and Spin on In-Line Skates?

You may be already be cynically thinking, 'Yeah, sure; like I'm going to be able to get out there and perform advanced maneuvers – *right.*' And, after all, what is the attraction here? Why even bother to learn jumps and spins on in-line skates? The simple answer is pure enjoyment; you will actually learn to do these moves! Actually, there are a great many reasons, but to list them here would be next to impossible. More to the point is that while jumping and spinning is really quite easy on ice skates, these beautiful and classic maneuvers don't come quite as naturally on in-line skates. Then why tackle these maneuvers? That's an easier question to answer. If you are an ice skater or artistic roller skater, there is something compelling about the refined dynamics designed into modern in-line skates. Put them on and they just naturally give you the urge to jump and spin, perform turns, dances, footwork, and more. Of course, the urge to do these moves can be limited by the fact you're on wheels instead of blades. While that can seem like a real frustration, the good news is that if you have the desire and the time, you'll find that just a little effort re-creating those classic ice moves can be marvelously rewarding and challenging. What if you are *not* an accomplished ice skater or artistic roller skater? Don't worry about it; you'll find that learning to jump and spin is just adding another satisfying dimension to in-line skating. Just take a moment to paint a mental picture: Can you imagine yourself gliding out to the center of the rink, performing a perfect one-foot spin, and seeing the look on the faces of those who watch? The surprise alone is worth it; you would be amazed how many ice skaters and quad roller skaters have never even been near in-line skates. When they get a look at what is possible, they're bound to be impressed! Although it's a kick to impress spectators, keep in mind, the main thing is simply to go out there and have fun!

You may even detect a large enough streak of talent to get

you thinking about entering in-line skate competitions. *USA Roller Skating* holds a number of such events throughout the U.S., and in-line competitions have even found their way into the big time; several events are now formally held at the Roller Skating World Championships. If you want more information about these meets, I've provided the address of the USA Roller Skating Association at the end of this book. You can also check with your local roller rink – the folks there will be able to tell you about their own artistic skating programs or club, and that's one of the best ways to find out about competitive events in your local area.

Note: I've made the assumption here that you are already comfortable on in-line skates; that is, you can stroke, stop, go backward, and glide on one foot. If you are not quite there yet, don't worry, there are excellent books available to help you get started. Can you tackle it? Sure, and you'll have a lot of fun building up your skill level. Harmony Sports, makers of the *PIC®* Frame in-line figure skate, has an excellent manual on the basics of in-line skating. That's the type of skate I personally train on and teach with, so I especially recommend their manual to those of you who consider yourselves absolute beginners who simply want to learn the basics. The manual is also a component of an exciting new training system called the GYM SKATE™ program that can be used at school campuses, in case you don't have a roller rink nearby. The GYM SKATE™ program was developed by Harmony Sports to interest more skaters in in-line skating, and I'll have a special section with details on it at the end of this book.

**PIC® Skating**

Another excellent resource is *Get Rolling: The Beginner's Guide to In-Line Skating* by Liz Miller. There is also an excellent web site related to this publication that will help all in-line skaters: Liz Miller's Get Rolling In-Line Skating Web Site. It can be found at http://www.getrolling.com.

You'll also notice that I often refer to classic skating terms, such as, *outside edge, free foot*, etc. If some of these sound like Greek to you, get a copy of the *United States Figure Skating Association Rulebook.* Some other reference sources are *Ice Skating, Steps to Success* by Karin Kunzie-Watson or *Ice Skating Basics* by Aaron Foeste for a complete explanation. Roller Skating Associations also have similar manuals. Also, at the end of this writing, you'll find a short glossary of basic skating terms—so don't feel bashful about taking a peek back there whenever you run into a term or expression you don't recognize.

You'll also notice that I've designed the training methods to utilize "toe-pick" skate-oriented in-line skating, meaning you'll probably want to consider the purchase of a skate which features the rubber toe stop, or toe pick, mounted on the front of the skate. In fact, you probably won't be able to perform many of the moves I describe without one. You may already have realized that most street style in-line skates have a rubber stop or brake at the rear of the skate, so how can you skate these moves on the pair you now own?  First, many of the moves I describe *can* be attempted without a toe pick, but remember, you really do need skates equipped with toe picks to do most of these moves properly.  In the next section, I'll help you get familiar with specific types and brands of skates available for performing the jumps, spins, and other maneuvers you'll learn.

Here's a suggestion:

If you want to try some of the moves described here that do require a toe pick, but don't want to purchase a skate especially with a toe pick, do the following:
Remove your front wheel and replace with a *PIC*® or with a wheel that does not move.  Then, you should be able to at least try the moves that require a toe pick.

## What Kind of Skates Do I Need?

If you want to do jumps and spins on in-lines skates, forget those garage-sale specials.  If you really want to get serious, you'll need to purchase a skate that will feel and perform as much like an ice figure skate as possible–that's the key here. Here's another big difference between your typical sporting-goods store skate and in-line figure skates: they're made up of two elements, the boot and the blade/wheel assembly. The two components can even be purchased separately, just like ice skates.

Let me loudly stress another *caveat:* Your boots must fit you properly. After you've performed some of the moves in this book, you'll be painfully aware of the reasons why well-fitting boots are crucial. So spare the ointments, the blisters, and the pain by purchasing the same quality boot you would want for ice skating. Boots must have a lot of support, and while custom boots are your best bet, their house-payment-sized price tag may put you off. Not to fear; reasonably priced boots are available from GAM, Harlick, SP-Teri, Riedel, and Risport. You might even be able to afford more upscale boots if you purchase used ones; just be sure to carefully inspect them for fit, condition and care.

In these illustrations, you can clearly see how the skate's frame is rockered or curved to simulate the way an ice skate turns. Note that these skates also have a toe pick.

A number of companies are now offering this type of skate: Harmony Sports makes the *PIC*® Frame, preferred by many ice skaters. Snyder Skate Company offers a similar model, known as the Triax Inline, and this skate is proving to be popular among conventional quad-wheel roller skaters. Recently, SP-Teri Company, a respected maker of quality traditional ice skating boots, decided to enter the field in this relatively new sport with their Artistic Frame. And the trend hasn't exactly caught the traditional roller skate makers unaware; Atlas, a company that makes quad roller skates, offers a skate similar to the Triax Inline. Note that some of these skates are made for indoor use, but the *PIC*® Frame—the type pictured in this book— is made to be durable enough for outdoor use as well.

Speaking of outdoor in-line figure skating, you can do these moves on concrete, but it's an unforgiving surface and can be dangerous, so save the wear and tear on your clothing—and your hide—by trying them first in a roller rink. The surface is smoother, more predictable, more level, and free of rocks, twigs, or other debris that could launch you into some unexpected acrobatics. If you do skate outside, wear full gear: helmet, wrist guards, kneepads, elbow pads, and long pants, not shorts. In a roller rink, only wrist guards are necessary, with other gear optional.

Wheels make a big difference--and with good reason, there's a lot of technology riding those little rubber doughnuts these days. For one thing, they're not made of rubber at all, but a tough and resilient urethane material; wheels are rated according to hardness, dimension and even the type of sport they're made for. For instance, you'll find that a smaller, harder wheel seems to make spins work out a bit better than some other types. You may also want to check out hard full-radius wheels, like the kind used by those suicidal teen acrobats you've seen sliding down stair railings in cola commercials. In my personal experience, a wheel with a standard elliptical profile will work fine. The *PIC®* or toe stop must be in good condition and the wheels should be rotated regularly. You should rotate wheels from side to side, replacing your higher-wearing middle wheels with the lower-wearing front and back wheels.

What about the size or length of the skate frame? That's important too; like ice skating, in-line skating is a linear kind of movement, and that means you depend on that wheel base length for needed support behind your heel. Check out the frame on a *PIC®* Frame or similar skate. You'll notice that the frame extends behind the heel, just like a figure skating blade. There's a valid reason for that extra length: it's there to give you an added reserve of stability you'll definitely dip into any time you prepare to enter and land certain turns, edges, jumps, and spins.

Free skating in regular in-line skates is like figure skating in ice hockey skates; it's possible, but somehow never comes out looking quite as good. It bears repeating; just as on the ice, in-line figure skaters need a toe pick and a blade that is rockered and a boot that fits, before attempting jumps, spins and other advanced moves. And don't chintz on the skates; you need the best possible equipment to get the results you're after.

Ready to begin! I'll start you off with some moves that will get you up and moving like a pro, right away:

# Pivots

Pivots are a fun and easy way to get you feeling in-control! Just place the *PIC®* into the floor for a forward inside pivot,

push with the other foot, and skate around your toe. Make a complete circle around the stationary toe. To do a back inside pivot, simply reverse the procedure. This move will make you feel like an expert skater almost immediately!

## Back Outside Pivot

pivots

L. Geubennaix

Now that you've amazed yourself by completing that first step, you're ready for a back outside pivot. This move will make you look even better, but it does require a tad more skill. First, practice setting your right foot down with enough control to put you on a good back outside edge, while extending your free leg back.

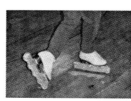

The "edges" concept here can be a little confusing to the uninitiated, but it's actually quite simple. Picture the bottom of an ice skate blade. Notice how it's not completely square? It's hollowed out in a concave curve to give each edge more "bite." Now, picture a skater wearing two skates, each with two edges; you have two inside edges and two outside edges; the better you control the angle at which they hit the ice, the better those edges work for you in these moves. Of course, in-line skate wheels don't really have any "edges" in the ice-blade sense, but ignore that fact, because when you are in-line skating, the effect is the same; leaning and edge control work for you, whether the surface is wood, concrete *or* frozen water.

Once you've gotten comfortable controlling the right back outside edge, make this edge trace a complete circle as you continue to reach back with your free leg. Finally, when you reach an angle of about 85 degrees, place the free leg's toe pick onto the floor and bend your skating knee a bit more. Continue to keep most of your weight on your moving skate toward the front wheels--this aids your balance--and make a complete circle around the planted toe. It's a bit like the way a tetherball twirls around its pole; your inertia powers the move.

Don't forget to bend the knee of the leg that is planted on the floor, and open up both knees as much as possible. After you've made one complete circle, straighten up on both legs. Be sure to keep the stationary skate's toe pick planted in the same spot; then lift up your heel. If you've done it properly, your feet should be at a 90-degree angle and your arms should be opened at about waist level just as you finish this move. Now rest for a moment and soak up the thrill; yes, you really did it!

12

# Attitudes

Attitudes are in that category of easy, pleasing moves that only appear difficult. Start off with a one-footed glide, stretching your free leg behind. Bend your free leg slightly, and put one arm up above your head and one arm out to the side. Make sure your free thigh is raised and turned outward. Keep your head up throughout. Next try the same body attitude, going backward. Finally, change feet and do the same move in the reverse direction.

# Spirals

Before you begin those most beautiful and elegant moves, the spirals, you'll want to put some practice into good edge control. Start by perfecting a good straight forward or backward edge, either inside or outside. Then, from a "banana" position, bring your body forward and your free leg up to the same level as your head; you should now be in a horizontal position. Keep your free leg extended and turn out the toe. After you get this one under control, you'll want to try making spirals on curves rather than in straight lines.

By the way, that curving spiral is the trademark of Olympic Silver Medallist, Nancy Kerrigan. I don't think the skating world will ever forget her winning performance that night; she has a unique way of holding her leg high and extended for an incredible distance, at least half the rink, while making a full 360 degree circle. Don't worry if you aren't in her league; you can still make a great impression performing this relatively simple maneuver. Just remember to push yourself a bit and practice this on both your good *and* bad foot! You shouldn't have any trouble moving into the backward version of this move; some skaters will even tell you it's easier to perform going backward. Just make sure to look behind you so you don't kick anyone.

# Lunges

    This move probably got its name because it bears an uncanny resemblance to a classic fencing posture. The drama of this one is sure to get attention. Like many other moves, the lunge is best gotten used to by holding onto the rail, bending all the way down on one leg, and putting the boot of the other skate behind you directly on the floor. Keep your back straight and completely stretch the free leg. It should hurt if you've not done this before! It may sound strange, but it's true; you are developing specific muscles to support the correct posture here. Once you're comfortable at the rail, you are ready to try it without a safety net. Now gain some speed and glide on a good forward straight edge and put the free skate's boot directly on the floor. Now, you are not going to go as fast as you might if you did this on the ice, but if you've built up enough momentum, you'll travel for quite a distance!

While we're on the subject of lunges, I'd like to throw in another fun move that I've named a **side lunge**. Glide forward on a curve. One skate should be on an outside edge, and the other skate should be on an inside edge. The skate on the inside part of the circle should carry most of your weight and your knee should be very bent. Your inside skate should be on the outside edge. Your other skate should be on the inside edge, with the leg straight and skate gliding behind. This move is another of those gems that may look difficult, but is so easy it will make you feel like an expert. It's sometimes fun to put one arm up and one to the side.

    Another interesting variation on the lunge is a move I call the **cross lunge**: Start the move like a side lunge, on inside and outside edges. Once you have a nice curve going, cross your outside leg over the skate that is gliding on the outside edge, as if you were doing a forward crossover. Place the skate that crosses over on an inside edge, and transfer your weight so that the leg on top (the one that has just crossed over) is bent, while the leg that is crossed under is straight. Most of your weight should be over the front knee (the one that is bent). Both feet (edges) should be gliding in the same direction. Want to make this move look really sensational? Try putting your arm on the inside of the circle, above your head (don't be afraid to really be dramatic), and put the other arm out to your side. You'll find some wonderful old pictures showing this move from the 1940's and '50's. It was a favorite move among some of the famous classic ice skaters of that era, so if you are looking for that Fred Astaire/Ginger Rogers appeal, this one is sure to work.

# Shoot the Duck

Bend both knees completely and squat down as far as you can go while moving as fast as you can in a straight line. Then place your right hand under your right calf and your left hand on your left knee and stick your right leg forward. This isn't the suicide maneuver you may be picturing, because if you fall, it's no big deal since you are already almost on the floor! If you don't fall, just bring your right leg back down next to your left one and skate in the dip position again and then stand up. Wasn't that fun? When you have complete control of the entry and exit, then you can try to perform the shoot the duck, bending down on one leg, with the other extended forward. If you have really good knee control, you can work up to getting up on one leg as well (assuming you are not like some of us in the over-40

crowd, whose knees complain whenever we attempt those under-20 moves!). Another, more difficult way to perform this maneuver is to add the element shown in the photograph above:

Extend both arms in front of you throughout the move. You'll be on your way to achieving that "Olympic" look. By the way, the real wild and crazy skaters will actually do this going backward.

## Spread Eagle

This is one of the more difficult moves. Don't feel bad if this one doesn't work for you; it is not one of those things everyone can learn to do. Moves like this tend to be the domain of people like figure skating legend Brian Boitano, whose amazing edge control and use of centrifugal force give him that almost magical quality of balance whenever he performs a spread eagle. Even if you don't think you can do it like Brian or Paul Wylie, it's worth a try anyway.

First start out at the practice rail for this one. Place your feet right next to the boards, turned out, and then push your hips and rear all the way into the rail. Hold this position for as long as you can stand it. Next, move away from the rail slightly --still holding on-- and try to hit the same position on outside edges. You can push your feet out at once, or you can stand on one foot, parallel to the rail, and move it forward, and then put the heel of your other foot down in line with the other foot, and then push your toes out. Now try moving yourself alongside the rail. Next, move away from the rail and try some inside spread eagles. Remember to place the heels of each skate in line with each other. Now try what you did at the rail on outside edges. It might take several tries before you can maintain going straight or on a circle. Once you begin getting comfortable with this exercise, try to push your hips under and keep your head up.

Photo courtesy of skater Nathalie Biedermann and photographer Eric Maurer of Visiomatics (www.skatetrix.ch)

A **spread eagle** *on* **your heels** (or back wheels) is a move totally unique to in-line skating; this is one of those moves that cannot be done on the ice. In fact, it appears to be impossible, period—sort of like when James Bond shakes the bad guys by putting his getaway car up onto two wheels to squeeze between buildings. Again, start at the rail, get into the spread eagle position, point your toes upward, causing your skates to go way up on each back wheel. Now move away from the rail and do an outside spread eagle; then, assuming you've worked up the courage, you can actually go up on your heels for a few seconds.

Keep your legs completely straight. You'd hardly believe it possible, but if your weight is distributed evenly, you should be able to glide for a bit. Some skaters just seem to have a knack, or a natural balance that lets them hold this position for impressive distances. Maybe you are one of them.

# Bauers

Photo courtesy of skater Nathalie Biedermann and photographer Eric Maurer of Visiomatics (www.skatetrix.ch)

Many skaters will be most comfortable learning this move from a very basic starting point, so here are some simpler methods of getting started with the Bauer position. In the following special section, you will learn more advanced techniques for this move. Remember, even though the Bauers look spectacular, they're really not all that difficult. This time, we'll again begin while standing at the rail. Put one foot right up against the rail, bend your knee, and stretch the other leg completely straight back; place it on an inside edge. Switch positions, and try out both legs. Then move away from the rail and try this position without moving, in the middle of the rink. Turn your hips and head and upper body in the direction you would like to begin your glide, i.e., the direction in which the bent knee faces. Once you have the feel, try facing the other direction. Next, try this move while actually gliding down the floor. Begin on two inside edges; there are some folks who'll pooh-pooh this method, but an inside Bauer is really perfectly acceptable—and just as pretty to watch, especially if you add some interesting arm movement. To try an outside Bauer, begin to straighten the move out by changing the leading leg--the leg with the bent knee--to an outside edge. Most of your weight should be on the front leg. Continue to turn your upper body, hips, and arms in the direction you are going. Once you've mastered the move, you can first lay your head back, later bringing back your shoulders and back, and even pulling your arms up over your head. Tonya Harding made the Bauer her own unique property by doing spectacular Bauers while capturing the title at the 1996 United States Figure Skating Championships. It's too bad that the controversies surrounding her off-ice performances overshadowed her strengths in this move. Many remember how she held superb leg and arm extensions and flowed down the entire length of the rink.

I'm inserting a special section on doing spread eagles and Bauers written by my friend Marion Ennis Curtis. She is an expert on doing these moves. Enjoy!

# Spread Eagles and Bauers
## by Marion Ennis Curtis

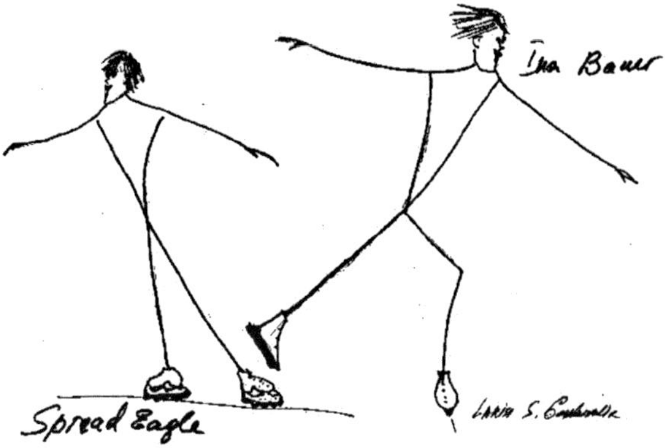


A spread eagle is an awesome, graceful edge move that can be done on both the inside and outside edges. This move can be held for a long period of time, exuding a fluid beauty, allowing the arms and head to move and create mood and symmetry in a variety of ways. You can go for the energy of a jazzy look, or move with grace in a balletic flow. The Bauer is a move similar to a spread eagle but more advanced. It was named for Ina Bauer, a famous ice skater who invented and popularized the move by superbly performing it for many years in the Ice Follies. All these moves require an "open-hip" position. To understand and feel this "open position," do the following exercise: Stand at the skating rail, toes facing the rail. Pivot your right knee to the extreme right, placing the heel of your right skate next to the heel of the left skate and forming a "V" position with both skates on the floor. Feel your right hip as you perform the exercise, and you will notice it has changed from a "closed" position to an "open position." Now practice with the left side.

The elementary spread eagle is performed on the inside edges. This move can be done in either direction, but for instructional purposes below, we will concentrate on technique for the spread eagle in a clockwise direction. Glide in a slight arc on both feet, skating with the knees slightly bent and arms out to the sides. Keeping control of the arms (do not let them fly around), open out the right hip (over the trailing foot) so that the skate is now on an inside edge. As you achieve this position, straighten both skating knees and arms. The arms should be parallel with your skates, and pressed down as if on a table in front of you. Both skates are on an inside edge. Maintain the position as long as possible in a wide clockwise arc. To exit the move, close the left hip and glide on two parallel flats backward, arms extended to the sides and slightly in front, in a comfortable manner.

After mastering the inside spread eagle, you may progress to the outside version. This move will be described going in a counterclockwise direction. The outside spread eagle entrance can be accomplished in two ways. The easier method begins with a slight swing with the right leg to aid in obtaining the proper outside edge upon setting the foot down. First practice the move with the aid of the rail. Stand facing the rail. Grasp the rail and place your feet in the spread eagle position. Make sure both skates are on an outside edge. Tuck your seat underneath you and press your hips forward as far as possible. Keep legs and back straight, head looking forward.

After this position is mastered, you can perform the move on the skating floor. On both feet, glide forward in a large arc in a counterclockwise direction. Lift the right leg in front (the skating direction), knee straight, keeping the left skate on an outside edge. The left arm should be parallel with the skating foot, right arm extended to the back. While still moving in a counterclockwise direction, swing the right leg to the back. As the right leg passes the torso, open the right hip and then drop the right foot on the skating floor on an outside edge. Keep the knees straight, arms parallel with your skates, and head looking forward. Hold this position as long as possible. To exit, you can lean forward slightly and change to inside edges in a clockwise direction and complete the move as an inside spread eagle, or you can straighten out your move by leaning forward and then closing your left hip, exiting backward on two feet.

When you have accomplished the outside spread eagle, you are ready to learn the unique and beautiful Bauer. The Bauer move uses the same open-hip position as the spread eagle but is usually performed with the leading skate on the flat or outside edge while the trailing foot is on an inside edge. It is mostly executed in a straight line, sometimes using the entire length of the rink for dramatic effect. Various arm and head positions can be done, depending on the desired look the skater wants to achieve.

The basic Bauer entrance is similar to an outside spread eagle. Skate around the far end of the rink counterclockwise. As you round the corner, begin the move by gliding on the left skate on the outside edge, left arm pressed forward, and right arm extended to the back. Lift the right leg in front (the moving direction), right knee straight, keeping the left skate on an outside edge and slightly bent. While still moving in a counterclockwise direction, swing the right leg to the back. As the free (right) leg swings past the torso, the move becomes a straight line rather than the arc for the spread eagle. The skating (left) foot transfers to a flat. Open the right hip and fully extend the right leg to the rear and drop it on the floor on an inside edge. The torso is straight and body weight is distributed evenly between both legs. Bend the left (leading) leg as much as you are able and tuck your seat way under. The key is getting into the straight-line Bauer position before you set your right foot down, then gliding down the length of the rink and holding that beautiful position. Add arm movements as desired. You may exit the Bauer with a left outside three turn and then glide backward on the right outside edge.

The mastery of these edge moves will enable you to add line and beauty to your skating. You will also have some long, dramatic moves you can use in your performance that will add interest to your routine while achieving strength and control in the lower body muscles. With practice, you will begin to feel the wonderful dynamics of the edge of in-line and ice skating, and you will acquire that natural and smooth edge flow that makes the sport of skating so revered.

# How to Spin

Here is one move that is hindered somewhat by the limitations of a wheel skate. Learning to spin on in-line skates is not easy! Spinning on the ice is actually much simpler, to tell you the truth. On an in-line skate, it is essential to get up on the front wheels to be able to perform a decent spin. If you practice what I describe below, you should be able to perform this maneuver.

1. The easiest way to start is with a 2-foot spin. If you spin to the left, try to get the feeling of spinning forward on your right skate and backward on your left skate: It will feel like you are doing a forward swizzle and a backward swizzle at the same time. The right skate should have most of the weight on the heel, while the left skate should have most of the weight on the toe.

At the outset, I mentioned that most moves such as this require a skate with a toe pick, but you'll discover that a two foot spin can be performed in regular in-line skates—in fact, it is probably easier. Balance is crucial here. Keep your weight distributed right in the middle; that is, keep your weight right between your left and right legs. The right skate's weight should be on the heel, while the left skate's weight should be on the toe.

2. When you reach the point where you know you are skating backward on the left inside edge, lift up the right foot. Stay forward over the left skate, and you will find yourself making a small back inside circle, and you should be spinning on one foot! The conventional wisdom says that attempting a one-foot spin on in-line skates is courting disaster, but here is where a pick-type in-line skate makes things interesting; these moves are cutting-edge at the moment, so you might as well give them a try. Then you can bask in the glow, knowing you are a true pioneer in this sport!

3. After you have mastered this technique, try entering the spin on a forward left outside edge. To make this work well, you really need to enter the spin with considerable force, after which, you throw your left arm around hard and pivot up to the front wheels at the same time; that should put you into a successful, centered one-foot spin. At this point you'll have the sense you are actually doing a very deep left outside forward three turn. The trick now is to bend down quite low on the left knee, which actually helps center the spin. Your free leg has to follow the curve; think of it as a tetherball swinging around the pole on its string.

4. (This next step will really help firm up those tummy muscles; it's better than Richard Simmons.) Hold your stomach in hard, and remain over the front of the skate; then pull your free leg into your knee while you raise up a bit on the skating knee. If all goes well and you remain balanced, you'll now begin to pull your arms into your chest. Don't forget to keep your elbows up!

5. To exit, pull out backward on a nice back right outside edge by making a swizzle with your left foot and transferring your weight over to your back right outside edge. Turn out and stretch your free leg, and hold the edge, keeping your head up. You'll need to push hard as you exit the spin. You've probably noticed that you are feeling pretty dizzy right about now. To prevent vertigo, focus on a stationary object, like the high price of Milk Duds on the snack bar sign.

6. Here's a bit of an add-on to give you some extra style. Try the spin from clockwise back crossovers or from a tight turning, sharp right back outside edge. I have found that the entry from the sharp back outside edge a bit easier than the traditional back crossover entry that is done on the ice.

## Sit Spin

Photo courtesy of skater Nathalie Biedermann and photographer Eric Maurer of Visiomatics (www.skatetrix.ch)

Once you have mastered the one-foot spin, try the sit spin next, instead of progressing to a scratch spin, as is commonly done. I'll get into those, shortly.

1. To get cleanly into the proper spinning position, first master the entry. One way to get your technique spruced up is by practicing lunges. Begin with your left knee leading, and then try a modified "twisted lunge" to get the feeling of how low you really need to go in order to get into a sit spin position.

2. You can practice some shoot-the-ducks here; they're an excellent way to condition your knees, which you'll need for getting down quite low.

3. After practicing the shoot-the-ducks, try doing a two-foot sit-type spin, using the same technique you would for an upright two-foot spin. Once you have mastered that, you are ready to try a conventional one-foot sit-spin.

Enter again with a very, very deep forward outside edge and whip your free leg forward. Turn the free foot sideways a bit so the heel of your skate doesn't catch the floor.

Now use plenty of effort and stretch the free leg way out; stay on the front of the skating skate, then pull your stomach in hard. Let yourself fall, which won't be a problem, since you are already down at floor level anyway! Next, try to get up by either pulling forward very hard over the skating knee or by pushing on the skating leg. Then, begin a spin in the upright position and pull out as you did with the upright spin.

I want to point out how vital it is that throughout the spin you stay over the front wheels and *PIC*® or toe stop, because it keeps your balance point vertical and you're less likely to conclude the spin in an uncomfortable and medically expensive way.

# Scratch Spin

The scratch spin is entered in exactly the same manner as a one-foot spin, but make sure your point of balance is far forward over the skating foot. Keep your stomach in and bring your free leg over your skating knee.

Stay in that position as long as possible and then slowly let your free leg and arms push down toward the floor as you finish the spin. To exit, pull out hard, or stab the floor with your toe pick to really hit the brakes.

Spins must be at the top of the front wheel and the *PIC®*. Yes, that is exactly where you need to feel that your skating foot is in order to spin.

It feels really weird to an ice skater to get that far forward, but just jump in and go for it! When I see beginning ice skaters go up on their toe pick, I know their spin won't work, but that's what you need to do if you are wearing an in-line skate with a *PIC®* or toe stop.

Pull your stomach in hard and make sure your chest is over your stomach.

As soon as you go even a little back on the wheels, the spin will end and stop. There's a certain place right between the *PIC®* and the front wheel that you must spin on.

Also, throw out the traditional back crossover entry ice skaters use with one foot spins for awhile. (You can try that entry later.) Instead, enter by doing a right inside three turn (if you spin to the left), then from that back right outside edge, push on to a very deep left forward outside edge on a VERY BENT KNEE, and use your left arm to enter the spin with much force.

If you want to pretend you are entering a sit spin, and then "chicken out," if you fall, you'll be so low that you won't get hurt!

Once you enter the spin as I've described above, you must hit that place right between the *PIC®* and the front wheel, and just like ice, you need to actually do a left forward outside three turn, so that you are creating back inside circles as you spin.

I know that this is all hard to explain without seeing, but please, don't give up!

# Camel Spin

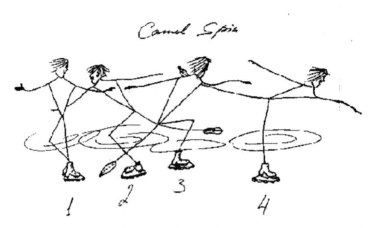

The camel spin is possible on in-line skates, but you'll sometimes run out of gas after a couple of revolutions or so—something about the friction of wheels being slower than ice.

Camels require plenty of space; you cannot perform them on a narrow sidewalk or similar location. Select an area with enough width; you need a lot of room for this spin. Begin by gaining speed by performing some back crossovers, then focus your attention down the middle of your skating area.

Begin by doing a series of one-foot outside three turns (toe turns) to build up enough rotation and momentum to attempt the spin: if you spin counterclockwise, do a left forward outside three turn, followed by a left back inside three turn. Use your right toe or foot to help you push into the forward threes. Use the same toe or foot to help turn from back to front, so that you can do several turns in succession. Let your upper body stretch out way over your left thigh, and begin to lift up your right leg so you feel like your entire body is horizontal. Don't lift the free leg too high; it will seriously upset your balance and you'll hit the floor with your teeth.

Once your body angle approaches horizontal and you have enough windup, allow your upper body to twist counter-clockwise in order to center the spin. Throw the arms around in the direction of the spin, and pretend that your arms are like wings. If that doesn't visually connect, picture your body forming a horizontal "T" with the skating knee bent. Now, rise up on your skating leg, and relax, but continue to keep your body and right leg horizontal and your arms stretched out, and you should definitely be spinning now! You may need to use your free leg to pump the spin to keep it going.

The goal here is to progress from simple to harder as you recombine elements, building toward the more difficult spin. Ideally, you'll begin with the upright spin to get the feel, then progress to the spin in the camel position.

## Change Camel Spin

Begin by doing some spirals for practice, remembering to use the leg you want to begin the spin on. For instructional purposes here, I'll explain this maneuver based on a left-foot entry. Enter on a forward left outside edge and let that edge almost complete an entire outer circle. I have picked up a tidbit from experience on this one. It's pretty hard to spin in the camel position for more than two or three revolutions on in-line skates, so here's a tricky bit of "cover up" to disguise the fact that your spin is petering out. Just switch to the other leg and continue the spin in a back camel spin position; you get a little extra oomph by changing the spin--it's good for an extra revolution or two! Let your free leg trace around an invisible table-height path, while your *new* skating leg makes at least one inner circle before pulling your free hip around. Exit by performing a short upright back outside spin, and deeply bend your skating knee to pull out.

# Change-Foot Sit Spin

After you've mastered this, try a change-foot sit spin. It's a straightforward change; once you are down in your forward sit spin, just exchange legs. Back spins are hard to maintain for any length of time, so be prepared to pull out quickly.

# Traveling Camel Spin

These are delightfully graceful maneuvers that make you feel like you are almost flying. They can add a jazzy touch to your artistic program because they can be used with other moves–you just whip around so easily! The entry is going to sound familiar here because a traveling camel spin is really a series of running threes in the camel position, ending in a short camel spin.

Begin by making a series of straight-line running threes (on one foot!) down the center of the floor; keep your back in a horizontal position. After they've been completed, you are ready for the big finale. Once you enter the spin, stay on a deep left outside edge, continue in the horizontal position, and simply allow the spin to whip around for as many revolutions as you can milk out of it. Once you lose the whip momentum, you can always continue spinning by pushing out on a straight inside edge (leading with your right arm) and continue with a back camel spin. Remember? This is just like the technique we discussed earlier, where you use a foot change to slyly slip in some extra revolutions. Exit just as you would any other back spin, i.e., by pulling out on a back outside edge with a bent skating knee. Olympic Gold Medallist Scott Hamilton is particularly fond of these.

# Traveling Back Camel Spin

Okay, now let's spice up the act by trying a traveling back camel spin. This time however, you'll enter by doing a series of right inside running threes. A series of right inside running threes consists of a forward inside three turn, followed by a back outside three turn; all on one foot. You'll do this in a straight line down the center length of the floor, as you keep your back in a horizontal position. After completing the running threes, start the final camel spin by getting on a deep forward right inside edge and pushing your right arm way around counterclockwise. Try to get at least one full inside circle in, and whip your left free leg around as if it were moving around a table top. Now, allow the spin to continue on a back outside edge for as long as you can possibly hold the camel position. Exit by doing a short upright back spin and pull out hard on your right back outside edge on a bent knee with the free leg extended. Raise your free hip slightly, and turn out your toe, and *voila,* you're done.

# Camel Spin into a Sit Spin

This is an excellent way to add drama, because this involves a lightning-fast change of position, guaranteed to get the attention of even the most jaded roller rink denizen. I should mention this is not an easy spin; the extra weight of an in-line skate makes it more difficult to perform than on the ice.

You'll enter this just as you have with the previous camel spins, by doing the running three entry in the horizontal position. Again, enter the camel on a strong left outside edge that almost makes a complete circle, and try to maintain the camel position for as long as possible. Now, briefly enter an upright spin position with the free leg extended high to the side and the free foot raised nearly to waist level, and then quickly sink into the sit spin position, so you can keep up your rotation momentum.

After spinning in the sit spin for two or three revolutions, begin to rise into an upright spin in the scratch spin position; alternately, you can also put the free leg to your knee, and then pull out on a right back outside edge. Remember, to keep the sit spin going you must get on the front of the toe of the skating foot while spinning. Ever notice how Olympic skaters don't waste any time getting from one position into another? Not only does it look clean and energetic, it keeps the judges from snoozing.

# Layback Spins and Attitude Spins

Take a breather here, because these will be a piece of cake by now. Enter the spin on a very bent knee, and lean way forward over the skate pick. Bend your free leg into the attitude position, and if all is still forward enough, pull your head back. First do it for only one revolution, and as you gain confidence, hold the spin longer. Arm positions are optional.

An *attitude position* is where the free leg is opened and turned out. Don't feel embarrassed, even if you think you look like a doggy encountering a fire hydrant, because that's probably the best description of how this should look when done correctly.

# Elementary Jumping Techniques

Back in the old days, jumps were rarely done, and when skaters did perform them, they were seen as frills; today the frills are gone and jumps have been integrated into the very fabric of competitive skating. Since 1948, when Dick Button performed the first double-Axel in Olympic figure skating to become the first American in men's competition to earn gold, winning has been impossible without jumps--and with good reason. As a skater leaves the ground, the audience is frozen in awed suspense, wondering whether he will touch down lightly or crash and burn. It's high drama, but artistic roller skaters had to await the in-line revolution before they could match the beauty of ice-rink quality multi-jumps. Today, with all the great equipment available to skaters, high and exciting jumps are easier to perform than you might think–and let's face it, they're the favorite of fans.

## Waltz Jump

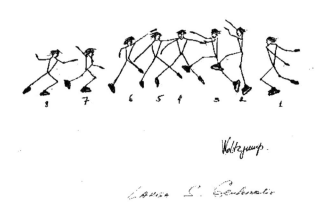

The waltz jump is an example of how in-line skates with toe picks have narrowed the gap, because they're performed exactly like a waltz jump on ice, which consists of a 180 degree turn in the air. Start your glide on the left outside edge, then roll up to the front part of the skate, and throw your right free leg through as you leap into the air. Make sure your arms do not go over your head as you jump. Don't begin any rotation until you are actually in the air. After making a half turn (180 degrees), land on your *PIC®* or toe stop first, then immediately touch down on your right back outside edge.

You can also perform this move on conventional in-line skates by landing on all four wheels simultaneously while traveling backward on your right outside edge. If you are used to performing this on toe-pick style skates, be on guard; you'll end up on your nose if you try to land on that nonexistent toe pick. Check or stop the jump rotation on landing by making sure your right shoulder and hip pull back slightly. Don't let your left hip and free leg drop, however.

## Bunny Hop

The bunny hop is an elementary maneuver that almost anyone at any age can do. The nice thing about doing these is that they feel something like a jump, so they're a great way to work through your natural fear of jumping. Start off skating in a straight line on a left forward outside edge, but heads up for the foot change. Swing your free foot forward, leap forward toward your right leg, place the right toe on the floor, and then change feet by pushing out forward on your left forward outside edge.

# Ballet Jump

You'll next learn the ballet jump, starting from a standstill. Place the left toe into the floor, jump from it with your left arm extended up, and then land on the left toe again. Lastly, change feet and glide forward to exit on your right inside edge. After

you've mastered this jump from a standstill, you'll be ready to do one while moving, entering from a right back outside edge. Go easy on the momentum here, please; crashes from this position can be rather painful!

# Tap Toe Jump and Mazurka Jump

Two more elementary maneuvers are the tap toe jump and mazurka jump. The beauty of these is that they make you appear to be jumping higher than you really are, so parents, get out the video camera for this one. You'll start off from a stand still, same as the ballet jump. Place the left toe into the floor, jump up, change to your right toe to land and glide forward to exit on your left forward outside edge. The mazurka is done exactly the same way, with a slight exception; you'll kick your right leg across your left leg as you jump. When you get comfy with both of these jumps from a standing start, you're ready to perform them from a moving back outside edge. These jumps also rate a bit lower on the crash/pain scale, so go ahead and enter them with more speed than the ballet jump.

## Salchow

Several moves I've told you about are more difficult on in-line skates than on the ice, but you'll be relieved to learn that the Salchow isn't one of them. That's because there is something about the way wheels stick to the floor on takeoff; you can control your edge with greater precision. When you attempt these, you'll quickly fall in love with the ease with which you can build and maintain rotation in the air.

You'll build up to them by first practicing a very straight left forward outside three turn. Start a turn from a left forward outside edge, transition to a left back inside edge, then stay very

45

forward over that left skate, and extend your right leg back. This edge must be kept checked, or under control, stopping any rotation at this point. Keep your left arm in front, right arm in back. To get the necessary rotation and spring action, bring the left shoulder slightly back, at the same time bring your right free leg and arm around, and then jump as if you are doing a waltz jump while moving down the floor. (Take some time to re-read that description; this is a somewhat complex jump to teach.) It is best to do this whole sequence in a straight line, as if you are jumping on a balance beam. You will need to go up on the front wheels and launch slightly from your toe pick to get some lift. Oh, and remember how your dad taught you to lift objects with your legs, not your back? Well, don't forget to bend your knees on the takeoff and landing.

## Toe Loop or Mapes Jump

The toe loop or Mapes jump represents the next level of achievement, without throwing too much difficulty at you; they're not too hard and you'll enjoy the pole vault effect as it launches you skyward.

The takeoff must be made from an almost flat right back outside edge. Start with a back one foot glide entry; begin the back one foot glide in a straight line. If your natural rotation is counterclockwise, begin by gliding backward on your right foot. Keep your left arm and foot in front. As you stay on that line, move your left leg to the rear and place your left toe into the floor behind you; spring off it, kicking your free leg through in a straight line, rotating 180 degrees in the air, much as you would in a waltz jump. Remember to use your left arm to help you in the takeoff by pulling it back around you when you spring off the toe. What you get feels something like a toe-waltz jump. Ice skaters might sneer because a toe-waltz jump on the ice isn't considered kosher, but we're still innovating and perfecting in-line figure skating, so to me it is perfectly acceptable on wheels.

Now, let's try it again, this time with a new entry: A right forward inside three turn in a straight line. Try not to lose momentum after the completion of the turn; believe me, you'll need it in order to jump nice and high.

Think of putting your weight toward the heel as you take off. That way you won't slow down at all; the move will continue to flow as you plant your toe stop in the floor for the jump. Land in the same nice checked position as in the waltz jump or Salchow.

## Toe Walley

The toe walley may be easier for some people, but basically is done exactly like a toe loop or Mapes jump, with the takeoff from a back inside edge, rather than a back outside edge. Two takeoff methods work. The first is similar to a toe walley on the ice. Begin a forward outside three turn, take a wide step onto the back inside edge of the other foot, then "pick" with your other toe and jump, traveling in a straight line, just as you do in a toe loop. You can also try the takeoff method that comes from roller skating. Approach the jump from back crossovers on a diagonal course toward a corner. Glide on the inside edge of the outside skate, keeping your free leg in front as you glide backward. Then bring the free foot back, and at the same time rotate your hips and shoulders counterclockwise, then "pick" with the free foot, as in a toe loop. After you pick, kick out like a waltz jump with the other leg (the leg that was doing the gliding) and jump 180 degrees in the air, landing on that same foot and traveling backward on an outside edge.

# Loop Jump

By now, you are probably itching to try your first full-revolution jump, and that means a loop jump. Full-turn jumps are the latest trend on in-line skates, guaranteed to impress, and you'll be doing them *backward*, to boot! The critical thing to remember here is that you don't want your skate to slip out from underneath you. That's why you'll enter this jump from a very straight back outside edge. Don't let your skate edge curve as you jump; instead, use your left shoulder to help you rotate. (Your goal here is to rotate counterclockwise through 360 degrees in the air.) Again, I want to emphasize the importance of balance; stay forward over the front wheels. It is best to keep your free leg in front throughout so that you land in exactly the position you were in before jumping. I know it seems like a lot to remember, but be sure to keep your arms in control, not letting them get over your head. Once you've landed, pull out exactly as you would from a spin.

# Walley

As soon as you're ready to raise the level of difficulty a notch, the Walley is your next jump. The Walley is similar to a loop jump, but with a back inside edge takeoff. Try it at the rail first: Stand on a back inside edge; then, instead of leaving your free leg in front, bring the free foot right next to the skating foot and lift it up slightly. Now jump 360 degrees counterclockwise in the air. Land on a back outside edge, exactly as in a loop jump, waltz jump, or Salchow.

Ready to move away from the rail for the real thing? Try doing an edge pull, that is, a back *outside* edge that pulls into a back *inside* edge. This move takes some practice and requires bending the skating knee hard, rising as the edge makes the transition, and then bending again. Bring the free foot into the skating foot, jump a full revolution in the air (toward the free foot), and then land on a back outside edge, skating knee bent, free foot extended back. Keep your hips and shoulders level throughout the move. You can also enter a Walley from a three turn, then a back inside wide-step, exactly the same as a toe Walley, but don't use your toe. This entry may be easier for you than the edge pull I've described above.

# Flip Jump and Lutz

The flip jump and Lutz are very impressive full-revolution jumps because your feet move like lightning due to the pole-vaulting effect the toe pick gives. It's easiest to progress toward these jumps in stages. Begin by doing half flips and half Lutzes to build your *PIC®* or toe stop skills. Don't rush; start out slowly.

**Half flip**: To do a half flip, enter with either a left outside three turn or a right mohawk so you are going backward on a left inside edge. "Pick" with the right toe, jump counterclockwise a half revolution, land on the left toe, and exit on the right forward inside edge. To finish: Make sure you do the jump in a straight line. As you land, continue in the straight line, gliding forward in a "checked" position, with the left arm in front and the right arm in back.

**Half Lutz:** Begin this jump clockwise, entering from back crossovers. The key here is to take off on an outside edge instead of an inside edge, but spring up on your *PIC®* and perform the jump exactly as you would a half flip. If you do it right, you'll trace an "S" pattern on the floor.

# Split Jump

Photo courtesy of skater Nathalie Biedermann and photographer
Eric Maurer of Visiomatics (www.skatetrix.ch)

Before you go full-bore into a 360 degree flip jump or Lutz,
you may feel more comfortable practicing two more transition
jumps, the **split jump and split Lutz**. These should feel
familiar already, because they're the same as the half jumps,
except that you'll scissor-split your legs by leaping forward in a
scissoring motion. These jumps have that wonderful quality of
being relatively easy, while spectacular to watch! After you
"pick" with the right toe, turn and leap towards your left leg,
land on the left toe, and push out forward on the right inside
edge. Keep at it until you are confident: then you can move on
to the full jumps.

You should definitely begin learning to perform the flip and Lutz slowly and carefully. There is some risk of toe pick slippage, I've noticed, so when you notice significant wear on your *PIC*®, it's crucial to adjust or rotate it for proper floor contact. Enter these jumps just as you entered the half flip or half Lutz, but add rotation to achieve a full revolution in the air.

1    2    3    4    5         6

*Lutz*

Land on your right back outside edge on a soft slightly bent knee with your free leg stretched and arms extended out. While you are still in the air, your arms should be pulled in close to your chest. When doing the full Lutz, I've noticed that you don't need to bend down quite as hard in preparation as you would on ice.

We have now advanced by degree of skill through the major jumps, but that's not the end of the story. Think of jumps as elements which can themselves be combined into artistic routines in an overall competitive program. Marion Curtis has some excellent ideas for this:

# Style Strategies: Combining Jumps and Moves by Marion Ennis Curtis

As you learn basic and even advanced moves, you'll soon want to apply those skills in a creative program. Even if you'll never enter a competition, you can add variety, difficulty, and excitement to your skating by putting it all together in an expression of artistry and skill.

Combination jumps are simply a series of two or more jumps performed without a change of foot. Many competitions have been decided in a skater's favor because the winning program contained combination jumps instead of single jumps! For clarity, this section will deal with jumps that rotate (turn) in a counterclockwise direction, noted in parenthesis. Keep in mind that if your in-line skates do not have a toe stop at the front of the wheel assembly, you will not be able to readily use your toe for jump takeoffs. In this event, you may want to begin your combinations with a waltz/loop jump and skip the section discussing toe loops.

Let's begin the art of mastering combination jumps by attempting an elementary combination, and for that I've chosen the waltz jump/toe loop.

Begin with an ordinary waltz jump, landing on the (right) back outside edge, and then attempt the toe loop by extending the free (left) leg behind. You are then ready to spring off your free (left) toe, just as you would for an ordinary toe loop. Stretch the free leg back as far as you are able before the tapping of the toe to begin the second jump; complete the toe loop as usual. The key to completing the second jump is to take your time between jumps and do the combination in a relatively straight line to avoid swinging too far and over-rotating the toe loop. Imagine a spinning top sailing over the edge of a table and hitting the floor and you'll get the picture.

After you feel secure with the waltz jump/toe loop, you can attempt various other combinations that end with a toe loop. Two of these are the Salchow/toe loop and the toe loop/toe loop--just apply the same technique you would in a waltz jump/toe loop combination.

Progressing to more difficulty, you can master the waltz jump/loop combination. Begin with the waltz jump. The key in preparing for the second jump (the loop) is to land the first (waltz) jump with the free (left) foot in front. The arms are in a solid checked position, with the left arm in front and the right arm behind. You are now prepared for the entry of the loop jump; bend your skating (right) knee and spring off the landing edge (your right back outside edge) to complete the loop jump as you usually would. Don't rush; remember to take your time between jumps, and keep your free foot in front as you land the first jump. Other combinations using the loop jump as the final jump include the loop/loop, Salchow/loop, and toe loop/loop.

There are many other combination jumps. Some are more aggressive and difficult than those described above. As you grow in your skating ability, you will learn to master combinations such as the waltz jump/half loop/Salchow, half flip/split jump, half Lutz/flip, and waltz jump/loop/toe loop. Enjoy learning and creating your own jump combinations.

Combination (or connecting) moves are really the raw material used to create the artistic expression of skating. They are the "nuts and bolts" which hold a performance program together. To help you understand this concept, picture a skating routine set to beautiful music that merely consists of stroking around the skating floor in a circle to prepare for various tricks, one after another. The routine will end up being an uninteresting catalog of moves instead of a moving performance! By contrast, visualize a routine filled with the same tricks, but linked together through the use of straight-line footwork, circular footwork, jumps exiting into edge moves, or jumps inserted between edge moves. Really, the purpose of connecting moves is to add style and beauty. The good news is that they need not be difficult to achieve their purpose and you won't have to be an Olympic medallist.

Here are three combinations of edge moves leading to jumps to start you on your journey of creativity. The first is a forward outside spiral ending in a waltz jump. A second type is an outside spread eagle with a Salchow as your exit jump. For something slightly simpler, try a forward scissors/two foot jump/back scissors. (On ice, the scissors move is known as a swizzle.)

To perform the spiral/waltz jump, begin with the forward outside spiral and as you exit the move bend your skating (left) knee and position your arms to begin the entry to the waltz jump. Follow through with a regular waltz jump by kicking your free (right) leg through and springing into the air, rotating a half turn and landing on the back (right) outside edge. If you are not comfortable with the waltz jump, just do a two-foot turn and glide comfortably backward, extending the arms in any dramatic position you may choose.

Now you can attempt the outside spread eagle/Salchow, beginning with the outside spread eagle. Next, transfer your weight forward to the takeoff (left) leg and lift the other (right) leg off the floor. At this point the right leg will become the free leg. You will then be ready for the three turn, necessary to begin the Salchow jump. Complete the Salchow as normal. Again, if you are uncomfortable with the Salchow jump, you can do the left forward outside three turn, ending with a back right outside extension or even a back right outside spiral.

Photo courtesy of skater Nathalie Biedermann and photographer Eric Maurer of Visiomatics (www.skatetrix.ch)

To complete the scissors combination, just do one forward scissor. Keep arms to the sides. After the scissor is done, position the left arm forward and right arm back. Keeping your feet parallel and facing forward bend your knees. Then jump to the right (counterclockwise) a half turn, landing on both feet backward. The arms will not move out of their original position, so only the torso rotates 180 degrees. Keep your knees soft to absorb the blow of the landing. Now that the two-foot jump is completed, glide comfortably straight backward on both feet with the arms out to the sides and perform the back scissors. If you are uncomfortable with the two-foot jump, just perform a two-foot turn instead.

Here are some more ideas to help spark the choreographic gift in you: a lunge into a spiral (with no foot change, this will take all the strength your knees can muster), lunge/waltz jump, or even a back outside pivot that turns forward into a two-foot spin.

Learning combinations can be challenging and yet they can be relatively easy to perform, enhance your creativity, add interest to musical programs, increase your aerobic activity, and help you develop more solid control of your jumps and edges. With your imagination, you can create and combine moves to produce your own signature style and skating mood. And that's the great news about staying in shape on skates. The exercise you are getting will seem almost effortless as you enjoy creating new varieties of moves you can perform to your favorite music.

Now that Marion has whetted your appetite for exciting multi-jump combinations and connecting moves, let's get right into some instruction on some primary jump combinations you can learn to do right now. You'll find that most of these are somewhat similar, but we'll gradually go from the easiest to the more difficult.

## Jump Combinations

Here's the game plan: We'll start off with some "simple" semi-revolution combinations, beginning with the waltz jump/toe loop. Following the method Marion described above, begin the toe loop, right out of the waltz jump landing. Progress to a Salchow/toe loop, then a toe loop/toe loop, loop/toe loop, flip/toe loop, and finally the Lutz/toe loop.

Next, you'll perform a loop/loop combination. Remember not to stretch out after the first loop jump and keep the landing leg quite straight. A waltz jump/loop combination is an alternative jump that's just as stylish, and you just might find it is easier to perform. Just remember to leave your free leg in front after the waltz jump landing.

# Falling Leaf Jump and Half Loop Jump or Euler Jump

One Half Loop

I want to briefly add two new jumps: the falling leaf jump and half loop jump or Euler jump. They're important; trust me. These jumps not only enhance your program as connecting jumps, they are simple and relatively easy to do. I'll give away a trade secret: half loops or Eulers look much more difficult than they really are, so you'll get lots of ooh/ahh power to impress family and friends. Enter a falling leaf on a deep right back outside edge. Let your left leg naturally sweep outward and leap toward it onto your left toe; change feet, exiting on a forward right inside edge. Check, or stop the rotation, by pulling your left arm in front and pulling your right arm back. Extend your left free leg slightly into the inner part of the circle, and pull your hips forward.

Ready to try two in a row? It's easy: Begin by connecting a couple of falling leafs, using either a mohawk or an inside three turn. If you do the three turn, make sure you leave your free leg in front as you jump.

Notice how the similarities between these moves help you pick them up more easily; the half loop or Euler is done from the same entry as the falling leaf, but jump a full revolution and land on the back left inside edge. The half loop is actually a full 360-degree jump; *don't* ask me why it's called a *half* loop—perhaps because it resembles a loop jump but is *half* as difficult. Anyway, check the landing rotation by keeping the edge straight and your hips square.

## Inside Axel or Boekel Jump

Although this jump isn't done on the ice much any more, in-line figure skating is so new and creative, we're free to thumb our noses at the ice rink fuddy-duddies and simply enjoy performing this marvelous one-foot 540-degree jump. Begin with a forward glide on an inside edge. Jump 1½ revolutions in the air, and land on the same foot you took off from on a back outside edge. You will find it is difficult to not "cheat" (doing a portion of the rotation before takeoff) this jump. In other words, to make a clean inside Axel, you cannot turn around backward by doing even the smallest inside three turn as you jump. If you do turn backward before you spring up, you will have actually performed a loop jump. I find doing this jump helps improve my loop jump and also is a great exercise to improve leg strength.

## Axel

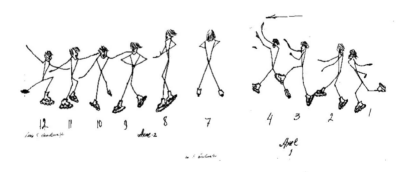

60

Axels are the most difficult of all skating jumps, because they involve an extra half turn of rotation, meaning a single Axel really has 1½ aerial rotations. These should not be attempted until you've mastered all of the above single jumps. Practice this jump on an imaginary line from a right back outside edge. Begin by making a nearly 180-degree turn around from back to front. As you step forward on the left forward outside edge, bend your skating knee--don't let your upper body get too far forward--with your head up; keep your free leg back with a soft-bent leg. As in a waltz jump, your free leg should pass through in a straight line as you jump. Once you are up in the air, pull your arms in to the right side of your chest, elbows down, and rotate 1½ revolutions in the air, landing on your right back outside edge. Pull out quickly right before landing and try to stay on the imaginary line, and before you know it, you'll be ready for double jumps!

# Double Jumps

Double jumps are moves that separate the casual skater from the serious competitor, not only because they demand precise control and competence at high speed spinning, but also because they are difficult to perform on in-line skates. Consider attempting these only after you've mastered the Axel. I recommend that doubles be attempted only by skaters who can already do double jumps on the ice or on quad roller skates. But if you are really committed to these, get a qualified private coach—ice or quad—and be prepared to invest considerable time, practice, and pain into learning these sophisticated athletic jumps.

# Advanced Spins

Once you've gotten comfortable with basic spins, you will naturally progress to **back spins**. Why? Because a finely honed

spin technique is a natural progression, an important stepping stone as you add jumps in your in-line skating strategy. A caution here: All skating involves some risk, but back spinning can be tricky. If you just want to impress your friends, this *isn't* the place to start. Naturally, back spins take considerable time to master, so be prepared to put in plenty of practice. And, since there's no time like the present, let's get started.

Begin by standing with your feet in a 'V' position. Leave your left toe on the floor, and make a large inside circle with your right inside edge. Do not pivot around your left leg, but rather keep your body weight over your right foot as you complete the 180 degree turn. This will center your spin over the right/back outside edge. Continue until you are pointing 180 degrees from the direction you started. This will give your spin just enough whip inertia for you to continue rotating on your back outside edge.

Want to try a different method? Enter the spin as if you are doing a forward inside loop; begin with a forward right inside edge, drawing a little loop or circle with your skating foot. After a full revolution on the floor, do a right inside three turn to put yourself on a back outside edge. Balance as far forward on the skate as you can, lift up your free hip and extend your free leg out to nearly 90 degrees. (On the ice the angle of the free leg is closer to 45 degrees--quite a difference!)

Whichever entry you choose, your exit will be the same. To pull out, bend your skating knee, rapidly and firmly extend your free leg back, turning your foot outward. Personally, I've come to the conclusion that I have to constantly monitor the position of my right arm, otherwise I have a hard time maintaining correct balance in a back spin. Of course you're now asking what your correct arm position is supposed to be. Well, here it is: Confirm that your the arm is in front, but at a slight downward angle, or as sure as the tax man comes, you can count on falling out of the spin every time.

Another tidbit you ice skaters will discover, as I did, finishing in a back scratch position--the standard exit on ice-- simply won't work on wheels. Because you'll need to keep your spin wound up, put your free foot to the back of your calf, then pull out on the right back outside edge when you are ready and you'll get just the right amount of yo-yo effect. Trust me, this technique works quite well; besides, it's a blast to do back spins this way!

I'm convinced that it is essential to work on **back camel spins** at the same time as you work on back upright spins. Why these came to be called camel spins is unclear--perhaps someone observed a skater entering an *arabesque* position and made the connection; at any rate, it's more dramatic, more difficult, and more impressive; but the bottom-line is, it gets more *points*.

Start off by practicing your forward inside spirals, then practice an entrance into a forward inside loop with your body in that spiral position. Make a 'Y' position with the 'Y' facing the floor horizontally. Now, with your free foot turned out, you'll have to whip your free leg and hip around. Note: You'll have to do it with some energy in order to get any kind of rotation going. After you get the hang of whipping around fast enough to build spin momentum, hold the camel spin position as long as possible. Then turn yourself into the upright position, but place your free foot onto the calf of the spinning foot so that your legs make a triangle. I've noticed that this method makes the spin continue for a longer period than if you hold your free leg directly in front; you end up with better control, to boot. Pull out of the spin by doing a slight back outside pivot, or simply change feet and pull out like you would from a conventional one-foot spin.

**The mini-illusion:** Though it sounds like an amateur magic trick, it's actually an aesthetic prelude to practicing a back camel spin. Reach down quite far toward the floor, and push the forward inside edge a good distance around before you turn backward to start doing the back camel spin. If you are flexible enough, your legs should do a complete split, with your free leg pointing toward the ceiling or sky and your body vertical, head

down and touching your skating foot! This move impresses everyone and is so easy!

Do a **flying camel** exactly the way it's done on the ice. The whip effect produced when making a jump seems to make the back camel spin occur naturally. If you haven't done flying camels on the ice before, it's wise to start out at the rail. From there, practice jumping from your left toe to your right toe, with your free leg parallel to the top of the rail, as if you are jumping on a table top. Move away from the rail, and try the actual flying camel. Now, don't say I didn't warn you, because you *will fall* the first time you try it! For control, reach out to the side a bit when you land. Pull out in the same way you would in a back camel spin.

A **camel-jump-camel** is similar to a flying camel, but you can allow yourself to do a bit of a forward camel spin before throwing your free leg into the flying part of the camel. This move should help you get used to doing the flying camel, so work on both at the same time. Remember to jump with your skating leg. You can get a mental picture of how it looks by picturing yourself swinging around on top of your dining room table on your tummy (makes an interesting mental image, doesn't it?). That's one you definitely don't want to try at home, though.

**Flying sit spins** are fun, look impressive, and are really not that difficult. Start by entering the spin the same way you would

enter a sit spin, but before you hit the actual sit spin position, jump up in the air and land on a back inside edge on the same foot you just used to jump up with and then allow yourself to get into the actual sit spin position and spin. You'll probably fall, but it won't hurt since you are already "sitting." Sometimes I just allow myself to fall on this move and spin around on my rear! Move over, break dancers!

## Three Turns

Some good news to those of you who haven't a background among the lofty and elite who inhabit the ice figure skating world, because the dynamics of contemporary in-line skates is nothing short of incredible. These skates have done much to level the playing field between the hard-core ice crowd and the roller rink crowd, so take heart--you'll be amazed at the quality of turns you'll be able to perform on in-line skates. If you are an ice skater, you will find doing three turns and mohawks similar to ice skating, but you will still have to unlearn some ice techniques to get comfortable with the different feel and dynamics of in-line skates.

*Laisa S. Gandarvalie* 3-Turn

If you are an ice veteran, begin with a turn in your favorite or easiest direction. Personally, my best turns are my left forward outside and my right forward inside turns, nor do I have much trouble doing right back outside threes.

Tip from Marion: If you are working on forward three turns on regular in-line skates, don't perform the turn on the upper front of the skate, but rather keep your body weight over the middle of the skate for the entire turn.

The first thing to remember is that while in-line skates don't have a sharp blade, they do have edges. You can trust those grippy urethane wheels; they stick tenaciously when you lean—just like an ice blade. Begin by cutting a deep left outside edge and keep your weight--that is, the weight on your foot--over the front part of your foot so you can control the edge. Once you've gotten your balance point up forward over the first wheel and the toe pick, attempt the left outside three turn by rotating far into the curve. Use your upper body to help prepare for the end of the turn by actually rotating it in the direction you will face when you are finally skating backward. Don't forget to check or stop the turn by pulling your left arm way in front of your waist and holding the right arm back. Keep all weight on the front part of the skate.

To do the right back outside three, you will first need to practice holding long right back outside edges. Again, keep your weight over the front part of the skate. Now, practice rotating your arms outside the curve as you glide and you will feel a natural rotation develop. Prior to the actual turn, your center of balance must transition to the heel. Again, if you turn your upper body and allow it to aim in the direction it will face at the end of the turn, your foot will naturally make the turn right under your shoulders. Once you are on a right forward inside edge, it is very important that you put your weight over the outside of the circle as you pull your right arm back, and put your left arm in front of your waist to hold the check on the turn.

Now, if you are already an ice skater, the right forward inside three just isn't going to feel natural, at least at first, so begin by practicing and holding your right forward inside edge. This has to be a deep inside edge, again with your weight balanced at the front of the skate. Follow the direction of the curve, and again prepare your upper body by turning it in the direction it will be facing when you will be going backward. Make the turn with the body weight still on the front of the skate, and then check hard by pulling the right arm back and pulling the left arm in front of your waist. Don't forget to extend the free leg back and to the side (which helps with control).

Back inside threes are challenging but worth it, especially because they hone your edge control. Begin the turn on the back inside edge, then twist your upper body in the direction it will face when the turn is finished. You may be tired of hearing it, but I cannot overemphasize the need for balance. Hips must be directly over the skate. Don't be discouraged if you can't do this turn right away. Persevere--you'll get the hang of it!

# Mohawks

MOHAWK

*Louise S. Gearhart*

These elegant turns are pure action, with the feel of flight as you soar a graceful arc across the floor, but remember to practice proper edge control before you attempt one. The best practice method is short distance glides on forward inside and backward inside edges. The secret to doing this type of turn is balance, keeping your weight distributed properly on your feet. You should feel like you are placing your toes on the ground as you turn. Of course each skater will have an edge preference; my best mohawk is the right inside.

To do this turn, begin by gliding on the right inside edge with the right arm slightly in front, and then bring the left (free) foot to the inside of the right foot. Place the left toe down, transferring your weight to the left foot. You should be on your back inside edge with your left arm checked in front. Keep your body weight to the outside of the circle, lift up your right hip (which is now the free hip), keep your weight over the left toes, and check your right arm back.

# Footwork

I suggest making up a footwork sequence that includes one of every three turn, alternately on each foot. My favorite is left forward outside to right back outside; mohawk; cross behind, step forward on to the right outside edge; repeat the previous sequence, to the right. After you cross behind, cross in front on the left back inside edge. Then do a left back inside three into a right forward inside three; cross behind and repeat the previous sequence, starting with the right back inside three, then into the left forward inside three, cross behind, and step forward to exit. I know those are complicated instructions, but there is a method to the madness; if you do this sequence daily, you will master all your turns--guaranteed! (This sequence, by the way, is the official ISI Freestyle Level Four Dance Step Sequence.)

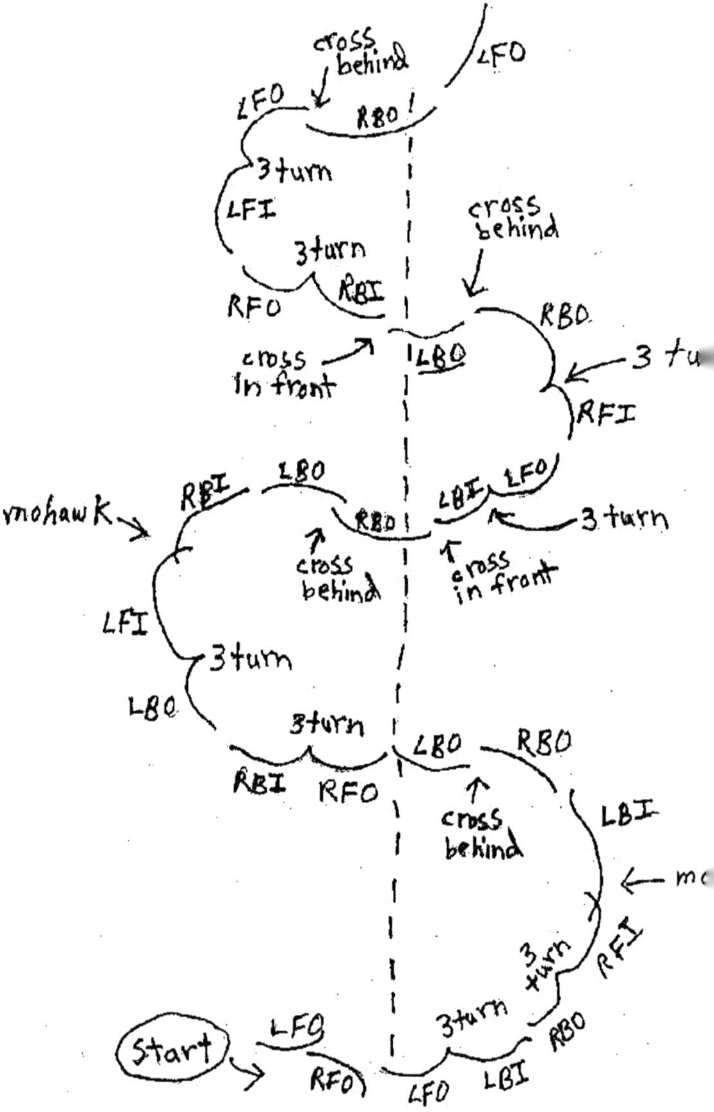

cross
behind
LFO
LFO            RBO!
3 turn
LFI
3 turn
RFO        RBI

cross
behind

RBO
cross            LBO            3 tu
in front                        RFI

RBI    LBO        LBI LFO
mohawk →  RBI          RBD    3 turn
                 cross    cross
                 behind   in front
LFI
3 turn
LBO                3 turn    LBO    RBO
        RBI    RFO                      LBI
                       cross
                       behind      ← m

                                   3     RFI
                                   turn
Start  →  LFO          3 turn    RBO
       RFO)   LFO   LBI

FOOTWORK

72

# Edges and Figures

Edges and figures just don't work that well on in-line skates, so don't be discouraged if mastering them seems unattainable. Here are some ways to practice them, however. Work on forward

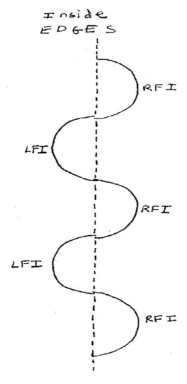

outside and inside edges with the free leg extended, as you lean back slightly. You can also practice **swing rolls** to improve your edge transition feel. Begin on your forward outside edge and let the free leg swing through to induce a shallow turn. Change feet and continue, making a series of shallow turns in opposite directions. Make sure you really bend your skating knee as you transition onto a new edge.

# Stroking

Stroking is good for stamina because it is still an effective aerobic exercise, though it isn't as much fun on in-line skates because they tend to have more drag than ice skates. Develop the discipline anyway and make yourself do it! Upgrading to harder skate wheels and better bearings helps; bearings are rated anywhere from an ABEC 1 to ABEC 7, but with anything less than an ABEC 3 you spend half your energy just grinding around the rink. Marion Ennis Curtis uses ABEC 5 bearings, which she says are actually reasonably good, but when pressed, she grudgingly admits they're still slower than ice skates.

# Back Crossovers

Back crossovers are not difficult and are an excellent aerobic footwork exercise because you get more workout per motion. They are done much like cross pulls; that is, each skate pushes and pulls. If starting counterclockwise, put the skates on a circle. Your skate on the inside of the circle should be on an outside edge, and the other skate should be on an inside edge. Now, starting with the left skate, make a "D" from toe to heel, sort of a half circle, keeping both blades on the ground. That's how you get the "push." Let that "D" pull over your right skate as you push your right skate under. Lift the right skate as you return the feet to a parallel position, then repeat the cross pull motion. There's no wasted motion; like bicycling with toe clips on your pedals, you get a lot of extra power because you are both pulling and pushing!

It won't hurt to add a quick reminder at this point. Like almost every other maneuver, these depend on consistent outside and inside edges. Part of the recipe for that is balance; in this case, staying back over the skate will help keep your speed up. Round out your practice by doing crossovers in all directions. Ever notice that crabs have one big claw and one little claw? Don't allow yourself to get trapped into having to go one way only.  Also, remember that in-line skates do have edges.  You will find that when you can actually turn the blade over you will have more control and more security as you skate.

# Forward Crossovers

Forward crossovers are really done quite differently than forward crossovers on the ice.  Again, put your two skates on a circle, on outside and inside edges.  Now, with the inside skate on an outside edge, push the outside skate (which is on an inside edge) into that "D" from heel to toe.  As the top of the "D" is completed, make the cross by crossing the skate over the inside skate (which is still on an outside edge) and pull that skate forward as it crosses under.  Make sure that the hips stay square.  Again, remember the push-pull principle; it helps you to keep your speed up.  Don't extend your leg as far back as you would on the ice.  To get the feel of the push-pull effect, first try keeping both skates on the floor as an exercise.  Bring the feet back to the parallel position each time a cross is completed.

# Stops

Sometimes it's the little things that get overlooked.  Imagine performing a textbook-perfect Bauer spiral waltz jump sequence, then scuffing off speed in an out-of-control sideways skid that ends in a wall collision, complete with the booming sound of heavy skates crashing into the plywood—kablam—right in front of the spectator stand.  Not a pretty picture to leave them with. I'll guarantee they probably won't remember the perfect combo you pulled off, because the last image in their minds was that embarrassing hog-on-ice finale. When it comes to achieving that graceful look you're after, stops are just as important as any other element.  You want to fool those who watch you skate into thinking that the stop is just part of an entire picture.

Drag T-Stop

The **drag T-stop** looks nice. Of course it's impossible to stop on an outside edge as you would on the ice, but on in-line skates, actually dragging the inside edge is a perfectly acceptable technique. If you desire, you can even stand in a nice "T" with the skates pressing on the outside edges after you've stopped, which definitely impresses spectators! I also find the **drag toe-**

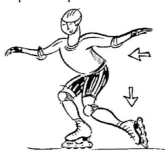

**Drag Toe Stop**

**stop** useful. Of course, you must have a *PIC®* or toe stop to do this move. Instead of allowing your wheels to drag behind you as you stop, let the *PIC®* or toe stop drag as you bend forward. Both the drag T-stop and drag toe-stop feel so odd to ice skaters since neither of these stops is considered acceptable on ice.

Using the toe stop on quad roller skates is standard, so don't hesitate to use your *PIC®* or toe stop when you in-line skate.

Drag Toe-Stop

A **hockey stop** is also graceful and presentable. Here's how you do it: With your feet parallel, turn to the left. You will want to push the right skate forward on an inside edge, in a small arc, as you turn 90 degrees; your left foot will make a MUCH smaller arc, almost a 90-degree twist. Leave the arms out to the sides and don't move them as you turn. Once stopped, pose and look straight forward and put some weight over your front skate. With practice, you'll look as good as an ice hockey player doing a hockey stop!

# Setting a Program to Music

Photo courtesy of skater Nathalie Biedermann and photographer Eric Maurer of Visiomatics (www.skatetrix.ch)

Up until now, we've worked hard on mastering a number of moves; now it's time to set a program to music. Select a piece of music that is about 1½ to 2 minutes long; classical music is always acceptable, and movie themes can be a popular and trendy source for music. Something with a definite, identifiable crescendo or change is a good choice since there are natural places to insert jumps or other dramatic moves. Select a place in the rink to start, and decide on a starting position. Almost anything will work; putting your toe to your side, with one arm up, or just standing in a nice "T" with arms down, are good choices. You might want to begin the routine with a pivot, bunny hop, or spiral. Take advantage of the connecting moves we learned, such as three turns, mohawks, strokes, and crossovers. Try a jump, followed by some footwork, then go into a spiral on a curve, transition into running threes, into another jump, followed by a spin, and finally some more footwork. Use of space in the rink is artistically important; don't skate in the same area over and over, and don't do one spin followed by another spin--it's generally not aesthetically pleasing. Make sure you know your music well. Practice your routine enough times to know when in the music to anticipate when certain moves will happen, and memorize your routine, every beat, every step. Finally, once the choreography is complete, end in a definite pose. Practice the program to music daily, and build up endurance to do it again and again. As you perfect it, you always have the option to add to it or change things around. If you do get a chance to perform the program in public, make sure you know it really well, and if you make a mistake, just go on to the next move and keep a smile on your face.

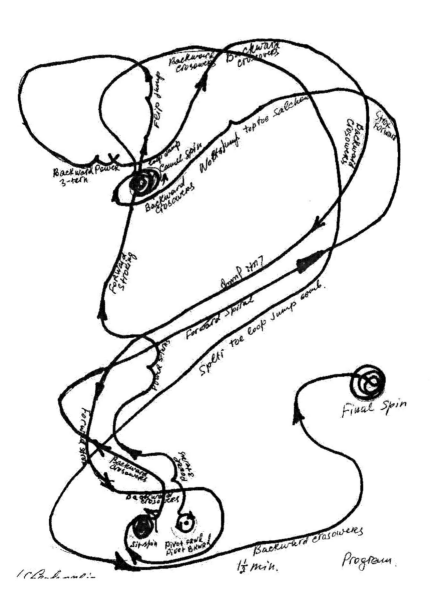

Backward Crossovers   Backward Crossovers

Flip Jump

Backward Power 3-tern

Loop Jump
Camel Spin

Backward Crossovers

Wolfsthung   top toe Salchon

Stroke Forward

Backward Crossovers

Forward Stroking

Jump into T

Forward Spiral

Split toe loop jump comb.

Power turn

Power turn

Final Spin

Forward stroking

Backward Crossovers

split jump

Backward Crossovers

Sit spin

Pivot Pawl Pivot Brawl

Backward crossovers

I.C.B...

1½ min.                    Program.

81

# Conclusion

In conclusion: Enjoy yourself. The explosion of technology has opened up all kinds of possibilities that simply were not available in the past. Never before has roller skating gotten *this* close to matching the elegance and the true feel of ice skating. Nevertheless, in-line artistic skating is a totally unique sport that awaits you with its own set of challenges and achievements. This is such a new sport; fresh competitors are already stretching the envelope with original creative performances; new competitions are opening up all the time.

You can enjoy artistic in-line skating almost anywhere: parks, outdoor skate parks, roller rinks, school gymnasiums and playgrounds--almost any level, smooth surface becomes an instant practice site (use your helmet and safety gear). Impress your friends and enjoy the challenge of being able to jump and spin on in-line skates. Have fun and Happy Skating!

# Glossary of Basic Skating Terms

*Axel:* The takeoff on this jump is on a forward outside edge. After jumping forward from that forward edge, the skater makes 1½ revolutions in the air and lands on the other foot on a back outside edge.

*Camel spin:* A spin done in the same position as the spiral.

*Crossovers:* This is the way skaters move around corners. On a curve, the skater crosses the outside skate over the skate that is on the inside of the curve.

*Dip:* The skater skates forward or backward on two feet and squats down as far as possible. The arms and rear should be level. A great exercise to get the knees going!

*Edge:* Skates have inside edges and outside edges. Stand with your feet parallel. Press your feet to the outside. These are outside edges. Now press your feet to the inside. You are on inside edges. When you glide on one foot, you must either be on an outside or an inside edge.

***Figures or edges:*** Figures are patterns done on curves. When you make a half circle on an outside edge, you have done a forward outside edge in a pattern. If you make two full circles that connect in a figure eight, you have done an outside eight!

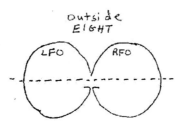

These moves are not easily done on in-line skates. If you do the above on inside edges, you have done an inside eight! If you do two half circles in a row, you have done consecutive edges. Don't be discouraged if doing edges and figures seems impossible. Even attempting these exercises will improve your skating in general.

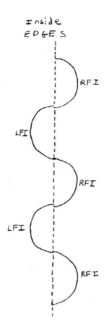

Inside
EDGES

RFI

LFI

RFI

LFI

RFI

*Flat*: If your skates are standing completely straight, not on an outside or an inside edge, you are on a flat. It is impossible to glide on one foot on a flat. Trust your edges to hold you. They will.

*Flip jump:* The skater glides backward on a back inside edge, picks with the other skate, jumps a full revolution in the air, and lands on the back outside edge of the foot that picked.

*Footwork:* When you put a series of turns and steps together, you are doing footwork. The possibilities are endless.

*Free foot, free leg, free hip, free arm:* This is the foot, leg, (or corresponding hip or arm) that is off the ground.

*Half loop or Euler jump:* The takeoff is the same as in a loop jump, but after jumping a full revolution in the air, the skater lands on the back inside edge of the other foot.

*Loop jump:* A skater takes off from a back outside edge, jumps a full revolution in the air, and lands backward on the same back outside edge from which he or she took off.

*Lutz jump:* Done just like the flip, but the takeoff is from a back outside edge instead of a back inside edge.

86

*Mohawk:*  A turn that is done from same edge to same edge, from either forward to backward or backward to forward.

*One-Foot Glide*:  Glide on two feet first.  Then transfer your weight to the foot you want to stand on as you glide.  Lift up the other foot while gliding on an edge.  Don't lift up the arms and also don't lift up the leg too high.

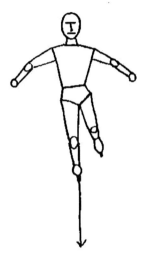

*Salchow:*  A jump done from the back inside edge of one foot to the back outside edge of the other foot.  A half revolution is done in the air. [Marion says it's technically a *whole* revolution]

*Shoot the duck:*  A fun move where the skater bends all the way down to the ground and glides on one foot while kicking the other foot completely forward.

*Sit spin:*  A spin done in the same position as a shoot the duck.

*Skating foot, skating leg, skating hip, skating arm:*  This is the foot, leg, (or corresponding hip or arm) that is still on the ground.

*Spiral or arabesque:*  A move done on one foot where the free leg and back are horizontal to the ground.

*Stroking:*  Moving from one skate to the other. This is what everyone does when they skate.  You can stroke both forward and backward.  To go forward, start from the swizzle "V" position, glide onto an edge on one foot, bring your feet together, and then push to the other foot. To go backward, start with your toes together, and then walk backward with your toes continuing to point inward. As you feel more confident, do a swizzle with one foot and then the other in sort of a "D" pattern from toe to heel.

***Swing roll***: A dance move that looks much like an edge, but the free leg is extended, and at the midpoint of the curve, the free leg swings through. The skating knee is usually bent at the beginning of the roll, and then becomes completely straight as the free leg swings through.

***Swizzles or scissors:*** Put your blades together with heels touching in a "V" position. On inside edges, push outward, then inward to make your toes touch. You should make the shape of a fish. You have now done a forward swizzle or scissors. Repeat by doing several in a row. Now try going backward. Reverse the process, starting with your toes together on inside edges, move outward, then inward so your heels touch again. As you make the move, make sure to bend your knees. This is a great exercise to get knees going.

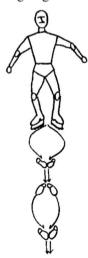

***Three turn:*** A one foot turn from either forward to backward or backward to forward, where a skater makes the pattern of a "3" as he or she turns. These turns are done from either an outside edge to an inside edge, or an inside edge to an outside edge.

***Toe loop or Mapes jump:*** A jump done with a toe assist. While skating backward on an outside edge, the skater picks with the other toe, then jumps a half revolution in the air like a waltz jump, and lands on the foot that did not pick. The skater should be gliding backward on an outside edge when he or she lands.

***T-stop:*** A position or stop where the feet make a "T" on the ground. The skater should place the middle of one skate behind the heel of the other skate.

*Waltz jump:* A jump that takes off from a forward outside edge. A half revolution is made in the air, and the skater lands on a back outside edge on the opposite foot.

## How to Figure Out Which Way You Jump or Spin

I always tell the following story to my students: I'm right-footed. What does that mean? That means that I land my jumps on my right foot. When I do a waltz jump, I jump off my left foot, turn in the air to my left, and land backward on my right foot. When I spin, I enter a spin on my left foot, turn to the left, and pull out of spins on my right foot. When I do a full revolution jump like a loop jump, I start on my right back outside edge, turn counterclockwise in the air, and land on my right back outside edge.

Most skaters are right-footed. I'm right-handed and right-footed, but my brother is left-handed and right-footed and my sister is right-handed and left-footed. Go figure. How do you decide which way is best for you? Well, at first try everything right-footed. If you notice that your left foot seems stronger, there is a good chance you are left-footed. Note the direction in which spinning seems more natural to you. If your left foot seems more stable and you like spinning to the right, you are probably left-footed.

A skater cannot jump one way and spin the other! If you prefer landing on your right foot, you must spin to the left and pull out on the right leg. You have no choice; otherwise, when you get to more advanced moves, nothing will work properly. For example, a good back spin is necessary to do loop jumps, Axels, and double jumps. Also, when you try to put a program together, the choreography will look lopsided and wrong. Even if you are jumping and spinning on in-line skates just for fun, stick to jumping and spinning in the same direction.

# Where to Purchase the PIC® Frame Skate and Related Products

**PIC® Skating**

The *PIC®* Skate Company - P.O. Box 219 - Malden, MA 02148 - U.S.A. - (800) 882-3448
Fax: (781) 324-4449
Web site: http://www.picskate.com

Rainbo Sports Shop, 4836 N. Clark Street, Chicago, IL 60640  (800) 752-8370

Or ask your local dealer for the *PIC®* Skate or *PIC®* Skate products.

# What Is the Gym Skate™ Program?

It is a program designed to provide instruction to students (grade levels K-12) on the basic skating skills in a gym setting at a nominal cost. The equipment used is a *PIC®* Rental Skate. This is an in-line skate designed to duplicate ice skates. It is safe, highly maneuverable, and easy to skate on. The skate is gym floor safe.

The Gym Skate Program provides:

1. Use of equipment for 5 or 10 days.
2. A curriculum and teachers guide.
3. Delivery and pick up of equipment.
4. Free use of skates for teachers and staff.
5. Skate instructors are available at a modest fee to aid the physical education staff.

The *PIC®* Skate Company
P.O. Box 219
Malden, MA 02148  U.S.A
(800) 882-3448:
E-mail: sales@picskate.com

# Where to Get Information on Artistic In-line Skating Competitions

USA Roller Skating
4730 South Street
P.O. Box 6579
Lincoln, NE 68506
(402) 483-7551
FAX: (402) 483-1465

# Take Part in the In-Line Jump and Spinners E-mail Mailing List!

This list can be found at http://www.onelist.com /community/Inlinejumpspinners.

It is an e-mail mailing list dedicated to those who are learning to jump and spin on in-line skates. Many of those who participate in this list own *PIC*® Frame skates or Triax in-line skates, and still others own regular in-line skates. Some of the techniques are similar to figure (ice skating) as well as artistic roller skating. Members want to trade information, explore new techniques and innovative moves, and learn about upcoming events, competitions, and clubs. This is a new and exciting sport with many possibilities. All are invited to join.

For more information write to superskater@writepower.com.

# About the Author

**Jo Ann Schneider Farris** began ice skating in 1964. In 1975, she won a silver medal in the United States National Figure Skating Championships and became a United States Figure Skating Association Gold Medallist in 1976. In 1983, she began her career as an ice skating coach, and has trained skaters of all ages and levels. When in-line skates came out in the early 1980s, Jo Ann and her husband, Dan, were among the first to buy the original Rollerblades, and they enjoyed all the attention the skates attracted when they skated on them in the streets, beaches and parks in California. In 1995, the *PIC*® Frame Skate was developed, and Jo Ann was one of the first to buy the product. She has spent the last few years working on learning to re-create everything she can do on the ice on the in-line skate.

She lives in Colorado Springs, Colorado with her husband and three children, Joel, Rebekah, and Annabelle. She teaches both

ice and in-line skating, and directs and coordinates skating programs at both the Ice Arena at Chapel Hills Mall and at Honnen Ice Rink at Colorado College. Jo Ann is a graduate of Colorado College, and holds a California Multiple Subject Teaching Credential from California State University at Long Beach. When Jo Ann is not coaching skating or jumping and spinning on her *PIC®* Frame Skates, she enjoys cross-country skiing, swimming, creating web sites, playing hockey with her son Joel, in-line skating outdoors with her family, and playing and singing with her husband and children.

# About Marion Ennis Curtis

Marion Ennis Curtis is a USFSA Double Silver Medallist. She has taught figure skating since 1979 and is a registered PIC® Frame in-line coach. Marion, who lives with her husband Bruce and two skating children, holds a California Multiple Subject Teaching Credential and currently coaches both in-line and quad skating in Morro Bay, California.

# About Larisa Gendernalik

Larisa Gendernalik began skating in Saint Petersburg (Leningrad), Russia, and competed in the National Championships in Russia. In 1979, three years after graduating from the Academy of Sport Science and Physical Education with a B.S. degree, she started teaching in the United States. She is Master Rated by the Professional Skaters Association, and teaches figures, freestyle, field moves, and choreography, and also arranges music for skaters. Larisa was on staff at the world famous Broadmoor World Arena for eight and a half years, and has trained many national competitors. She began drawing at a young age in Russia, and completed several art courses there. Larisa loves dramatic theater, music, ballet, and art, and she loves to ski. She now lives in Colorado Springs, Colorado with her husband and two children, Valerie and Alex, and her two dogs, Bazil and Forrest.

# About The Book

**This book describes in detail how to re-create all that is possible on the ice!**

JUMPS! Yes, it is possible to do waltz jumps, salchows, loops, lutzes, flips, axels, and double jumps on in-line skates!

SPINS! Yes, you can do sit spins, scratch spins, and flying camels on in-line skates!

**FOOTWORK AND MUCH MORE!** You can do about anything that is possible on the ice on in-line skates!

**This book will show you how!**

**Also included in this publication are excellent illustrations by Professional Skaters Association Master Rated figure skating coach Larisa Gendernalik. Several photos of in-line jump-and-spinners in action are also provided. Additional information is provided by skating coach Marion Ennis Curtis.**

What people are saying about the book:

*Comment from a reader:*
*"I highly recommend that you order Jo Ann Schneider Farris' book, How to Jump and Spin on In-Line Skates. It'll answer a lot of questions, help to get you started, and is a real encouragement. It's a great reference guide and fun to read (also has photos). Patti"*

**From Liz Miller, well-known California skating instructor and author of the books *Get Rolling* and *California Inline Skating*:**
*"Jo Ann has a warm, encouraging and very enthusiastic writing style, and she delivers what the book's title promises: information about the in-line figure skating discipline, gear, and moves. The gear section and glossary are also useful."*

**From John Petell, President of Harmony Sports:**
*"Jo Ann's book is a giant step toward exposing the fine sport of in-line freestyle skating, with its many and wondrous movements, to the public.*

**From Nick Perna, National and International figure skating coach and co-inventor of the *PIC*® Frame Skate:**
*"This book is well written and extremely thorough for this type of instruction. I think just about anybody who is interested in in-line figure skating techniques will be able to learn something new from this book."*

### *Comment from the author:*
*"I want to encourage everyone who in-line skates to consider jumping and spinning on your skates! It is so much fun. You don't have to be an advanced figure skater to jump and spin; on in-line skates, there are no rules really, so you can even create your own moves. Also, consider this: imagine how impressed your friends will be when they see you do a small jump, glide into an artistic move like a spiral, or see you spinning on one foot? They might want to try it too.*

*For me jumping and spinning on in-lines helped me remember why I enjoy skating. It is so challenging, and there's always something new to try. I'm never bored!*

*You'll find that learning to jump and spin is just adding another satisfying dimension to in-line skating. Keep in mind, the main thing is simply to go out there and have fun!*

*Jo Ann Schneider Farris"*
(To read more about author Jo Ann Schneider Farris and her skating family, go to inlineskating.about.com:
http://inlineskating.about.com/sports/inlineskating/library/weekly
/aa112999.htm.)

**So..........**
**Do bauers, spread eagles, pivots, camel spins, and much more!**
**Skate outdoors or inside a gym or roller rink.**
**And...................**
**Impress your friends!**

LaVergne, TN USA
30 August 2009
156392LV00001B/21/A